# The Sun Will Rise Despite the Darkness

# The Sun Will Rise Despite the Darkness

FINDING PEACE, LOVE, AND
HOPE IN JESUS CHRIST

*Jacki Tase*

All Scripture quotations, unless otherwise indicated, are taken from
the Holy Bible, New International Version®, "NIV®" Copyright © 1973,
1978, 1984, International Bible Society. Use by permission of Zondervan.
Publishing House. All rights reserved.

Copyright © 2004 Jacki Tase
Revised Edition 2015

ISBN-13: 9781519739902
ISBN-10: 1519739907

I am deeply grateful to my husband, Doug, who has always stood by my side and encouraged me to follow the Lord wherever he leads. And to my daughters, Carolyn and Christine, for the incredible love and joy they are in my life.

*Because of the LORD's great love we are not consumed, for his compassions never fail. They are new every morning; great is your faithfulness.* (Lam. 3:22–23)

# A Note from the Author

I BELIEVE WE ARE ALL searching for the meaning and purpose of our lives. It took me a while to realize I had been searching my entire life for what I now know. This searching forces us to make choices. Many times the choices we make take us far away from what we truly need. I took many roads and watched as friends took others. Because of this, I know there is always a hope that shines in the darkness. I never intended to write a book, but as I read scripture and wrestled with its meaning and implications for my life, I wrote and shared my writing with friends. I began to see the encouragement it gave them and how it helped them to see more clearly the incredible hope, love, and peace that are available to all of us.

It is from this prompting from others that this book first came to be. I have updated this book from the original version from ten years ago, changing the format a bit and adding devotional pieces. It is my hope that while reading this book over the next 85 days you will draw closer to the heart of God.

There is a place that we belong. I find it ironic that this place was the last place I was willing to look; I never thought I would find what I was looking for there. Maybe you have a feeling of emptiness within you—one you are unable to fill by doing more, buying more, or achieving more. Somehow these things are never enough for very long. Maybe you have a nagging feeling that there must be something more to life than this. Or maybe life is just so overwhelming that you cannot believe there is a light that can break through the dark place where you now live.

There is, but you must reach out for it. This book is about reaching out for hope. It is about wrestling with something beyond us, something greater than us. It is about finding that place of belonging. It is about the love, peace, and hope we so greatly desire and need.

I suggest finding a quiet place to read the page for each day. Start with what I have written, and then let that writing guide you to the only words that can give you what you truly need: the Word of God. There is space for you to write your own short prayer and a few reflections if you desire to do so.

I hope this book will encourage you, inspire you, and give you hope. For, at the end of the day, there is only one thing that matters: whether or not you know Jesus Christ. In him you will find the love, peace, and hope you so desire and need. In Jesus, you will find the place that you belong.

Blessings,
Jacki Tase

# Contents

God's Love · · · · · · · · · · · · · · · · · · · · · · · · · · · · · · · · · · · · · · · · · · · 1
The Greatness of God · · · · · · · · · · · · · · · · · · · · · · · · · · · · · 15
Grace · · · · · · · · · · · · · · · · · · · · · · · · · · · · · · · · · · · · · · · · · · · · · 21
Hope · · · · · · · · · · · · · · · · · · · · · · · · · · · · · · · · · · · · · · · · · · · · · 29
Truth · · · · · · · · · · · · · · · · · · · · · · · · · · · · · · · · · · · · · · · · · · · · · 37
Wisdom · · · · · · · · · · · · · · · · · · · · · · · · · · · · · · · · · · · · · · · · · · 43
Peace · · · · · · · · · · · · · · · · · · · · · · · · · · · · · · · · · · · · · · · · · · · · · 49
Guidance · · · · · · · · · · · · · · · · · · · · · · · · · · · · · · · · · · · · · · · · · 55
Letting Go · · · · · · · · · · · · · · · · · · · · · · · · · · · · · · · · · · · · · · · · 71
Change · · · · · · · · · · · · · · · · · · · · · · · · · · · · · · · · · · · · · · · · · · · 77
Faith · · · · · · · · · · · · · · · · · · · · · · · · · · · · · · · · · · · · · · · · · · · · · · 85
Feeling Alone · · · · · · · · · · · · · · · · · · · · · · · · · · · · · · · · · · · · · 89
Grief · · · · · · · · · · · · · · · · · · · · · · · · · · · · · · · · · · · · · · · · · · · · · · 95
When God Seems Silent · · · · · · · · · · · · · · · · · · · · · · · · · · 99
Obedience · · · · · · · · · · · · · · · · · · · · · · · · · · · · · · · · · · · · · · · 103
Purpose · · · · · · · · · · · · · · · · · · · · · · · · · · · · · · · · · · · · · · · · · · 109
Seeking God · · · · · · · · · · · · · · · · · · · · · · · · · · · · · · · · · · · · · 125

Following Jesus · · · · · · · · · · · · · · · · · · · · · · · · · · · · · · · · · 131
Fear · · · · · · · · · · · · · · · · · · · · · · · · · · · · · · · · · · · · · · · · · · · · · · 137
Strength · · · · · · · · · · · · · · · · · · · · · · · · · · · · · · · · · · · · · · · · · · 143
Trusting God · · · · · · · · · · · · · · · · · · · · · · · · · · · · · · · · · · · · 151

*The Sun Will Rise Despite the Darkness*

Lord, open my heart to all I need to know.
Open my eyes and ears to all that is necessary to see and hear.
Give me strength for all I need to face this day and
Courage and boldness to speak words of truth.
Hold me, so I may stand on this day.
Keep my eyes and heart focused on you, Lord Jesus.
Fill my heart with love.
Let my words and actions bring only glory to your name.
I understand I am here for "such a time as this."
Use me however you desire,
For you have paid the price for me.
My desire is to serve you alone.

*I have loved you with an everlasting love. I have drawn you with loving-kindness.* (Jer. 31:3–4)

Prayer:

Reflection:

# God's Love

*The Sun Will Rise Despite the Darkness*

Praise the depth of the love that Christ has for us,
For even until our last breath,
Christ is relentless in his pursuit for us.
This is a love we cannot begin to understand,
But it is here for us today.
Let us reach out and accept the great gift of grace and love
That is only found in Jesus Christ!

*For I am convinced that neither death nor life, neither angels nor demons, neither the present nor the future, or any powers neither height nor depth, nor anything else in all creation, will be able to separate us from the love of God that is in Christ Jesus our Lord.* (Rom. 8:38–39)

Prayer:

Reflection:

As we uncover our fears and our pain from wounds deep
within us,
It is our distance from God that prevents us from healing.
For in the abundance of God's love,
Weaknesses are found, and
Wounds are healed.
We are able to move beyond the pain,
Gaining strength,
Growing in faith.

*There is no fear in love. But perfect love drives out fear, because fear has to do with punishment. The one who fears is not made perfect in love.* (1 John 4:18)

Prayer:

Reflection:

*The Sun Will Rise Despite the Darkness*

It is easy to distance ourselves from the love of God.
When dreams are fulfilled,
Life is comfortable, and
All we feel we need has been obtained,
We do not feel the need for God's love.
Forgotten is the depth and breadth of God's love for us,
When we live only for ourselves.
The dreams are our dreams, not his.
They will not last.
Do you not remember
The times when you have gone astray?
When joy disappeared and
Dreams began to shatter?
When you were on your knees,
So desperate and in need,
You reached out and received
The gift of grace and love.
For Jesus did not abandon you then;
He waited for you to understand your need for him.
He waits for you now.
Turn back to Jesus:
Confess your sins,
Ask for forgiveness,
For your Savior will embrace you.
He is waiting to rejoice in your return.
This is a love that is difficult to understand.
We are not capable of this depth of love:
We are judgmental.

Our love is conditional.
His love is not.
In those times of comfort and self-fulfillment,
We do not understand the depth of our need.
Jesus is waiting for you.
Jesus has always loved you.
The question is, do you love him?

*The son said to him, "Father, I have sinned against heaven and against you. I am no longer worthy to be called your son." But the father said to his servants, "Quick! Bring the best robe and put it on him. Put a ring on his finger and sandals on his feet. Bring the fattened calf and kill it. Let's have a feast and celebrate. For this son of mine was dead and is alive again; he was lost and is found." So they began to celebrate.* (Luke 15:21–24)

Prayer:


Reflection:

*The Sun Will Rise Despite the Darkness*

In the deepest part of our soul
Lives a love that we cannot fully understand,
But it is our desire to understand, and so we seek..

*Ask and it will be given to you; seek and you will find; knock and the door will be open to you. For everyone who asks receives; he who seeks finds; and to him who knocks, the door will be opened.* (Matt. 7:7–8)

Prayer:


Reflection:

It is by faith that we begin to walk,
Alone and broken, lost and afraid.
Along the way we are slowly changed,
But it is not until we reach the cross and kneel humbly
in its shadow
That we begin to truly understand the depth of the love Jesus
has for us.
It is in this love that we are healed—
No longer lost, broken, and afraid.
Understanding we will never be worthy of this love,
Overwhelmed by his grace,
Thankful for this love,
In the shadow of the cross, we are finally free to love and be
loved,
To go where we are meant to go,
To be as we are meant to be,
To live as we are meant to live.

*To this you were called, because Christ suffered for you, leaving you an example that you should follow in his steps. "He committed no sin, and no deceit was found in his mouth." When they hurled their insults at him, he did not retaliate; when he suffered, he made no threats. Instead, he entrusted himself to him who judges justly. He himself bore our sins in his body on the tree so that we might die to sin and live for righteousness; by his wounds you have been healed. For you were like sheep going astray but now you have returned to the Shepherd and Overseer of your souls.* (1 Pet. 2:21–25)

Prayer:

Reflection:

The love of parents for their children is unlimited.
We share in our children's joy, hope, success, as well as failure and pain,
Walking together through good times and bad, smiles and tears—
Never leaving,
No matter how hard they try to push us away,
Even when they are unwilling to ask for and accept our help.
Always loving,
No matter what lies ahead.
God's love is in many ways like this.
He is with us
In success and failure, joy and tears,
No matter how much it rains
Or how large the storm—
Never leaving us,
Even when we are unwilling to ask for or accept his help,
No matter how hard we try to push him away.
We must remember who we really are:
We are God's children.
His love endures forever.

*How great is the love the Father has lavished on us, that we should be called children of God!* (I John 3:1)

*The Sun Will Rise Despite the Darkness*

Prayer:

Reflection:

Praise to my Lord God Almighty, who is my rock,
My foundation,
Strengthening the weak,
Giving faith to the fearful,
Comforting those in need.
Praise to my God,
Creator of the heavens and earth,
Who is all-knowing,
Infinite,
Uncontainable—
And yet can find me,
Understand me,
Know me,
Love me,
In spite of me.

*The LORD is my strength and my song; he has become my salvation. He is my God and I will praise him, my father's God, and I will exalt him.* (Exod. 15:2)

Prayer:

Reflection:

*The Sun Will Rise Despite the Darkness*

The Lord God Almighty is my king.
He leads me into territory unknown,
Prepares me always, in all ways,
Equipped and ready.
He leads me to new heights of understanding,
Guiding me, prodding me on to do needed works,
Understanding my fears yet giving me strength to go on.
You show me new truths and give me understanding;
No greater love and wisdom shall I ever need all the days of my life,
Till I kneel before my God in all eternity.

*My soul finds rest in God alone; my salvation comes from him. He alone is my rock and my salvation; he is my fortress, I will never be shaken.* (Ps. 62:1–2)

Prayer:

Reflection:

# The Greatness of God

*The Sun Will Rise Despite the Darkness*

Beyond my understanding is the greatness of my God,
With awesome power and might.
How often do I enter prayer without reverence for who you are,
Unable to see beyond my world
To the vastness that surrounds me.
How often do I enter prayer
Seeking only my desires,
Limiting the possibilities
With my doubt and fear?
Let me not forget who you are.

*Then I said: "O LORD, God of heavens, the great and awesome God, who keeps his covenant of love with those who love him and obey his commands."* (Neh. 1:5)

Prayer:

Reflection:

If we do not believe in the greatness of our God,
We will limit the power available to us through him.
When we try to contain him,
Try to understand him,
We reinforce our own disbelief and lack of faith.
He is larger than we are—
More powerful and uncontainable than we would like to believe.
When we believe in his greatness,
We must admit
That we are not great at all.

*How awesome is the LORD Most High, the great King over all the earth!* (Ps. 47:2)

Prayer:

Reflection:

*The Sun Will Rise Despite the Darkness*

Great is the desire to understand the power that stirs within us,
Motivating us to reach for understanding.
Great is the love that surrounds and protects us,
That we may see the glory before us.
Great is the desire to grasp what is unknown.
Great is our Lord Jesus Christ.

*Great is the LORD and most worthy of praise; his greatness no one can fathom.* (Ps. 145:3)

Prayer:

Reflection:

# Grace

As we begin to catch a glimpse of the holiness of God,
Understanding in some small way who God is,
The knowledge of our unworthiness is overwhelming.
It begins to shatter the image of who we believe we are;
We have been deluded by our sense of self-importance,
Our good deeds, pride, and accomplishments.
We justify our actions by saying they are in the name of God,
When beneath them all it was in our own name.
Before a holy God, we have nothing to offer.
We must look to Jesus's sacrifice upon the cross.
It is here we will catch a glimpse of the undeserved and abundant love of God.
How grateful we should be that this love has not been dependent upon us,
For it has not been given because of who we are or what we have done!
It has been given because of who God is and what God has done.
This love, this gift of grace, is freely given to all who call upon his name.
To catch a glimpse and
To see one's true self
Is to understand this undeserved love
And experience God's grace.

*For it is by grace you have been saved, through faith—and this is not from yourselves, it is the gift of God—not by works, so that no one can boast. For we are God's workmanship, created in Christ Jesus to do good works, which God prepared in advance for us to do.* (Eph. 2:8–9)

Prayer:

Reflection:

*The Sun Will Rise Despite the Darkness*

There is a gift—
A gift of grace,
Offering love,
Offering life,
Given through his son.
An exchange:
His life
For yours.
How freely we may take of it.
One question still remains:
Has the cost been forgotten?
So quietly pushed aside,
The pain endured
As he carried our sin and shame,
Left to die on the cross,
Despised and beaten,
Suffering and alone.
Has the cost been forgotten?
The darkness and pain.
The separation from God.
An exchange was made—
All for you,
All for me,
So that we may have
The love,
The life
Designed to be.
Do we truly understand the cost?

The gift we so freely take—
We were given life
When Jesus conquered death.

*Jesus called them together and said, "You know that the rulers of the Gentiles lord it over them, and their high officials exercise authority over them. Not so with you. Instead, whoever wants to become great among you must be your servant and whoever wants to be first must be your slave—just as the Son of Man did not come to be served, but to serve, and to give his life as a ransom for many."* (Matt. 20:25–28)

Prayer:

Reflection:

It is not until we realize how lost we have been,
How far we have run from God,
That we can begin to understand
How great the gift of grace truly is.

*But because of his great love for us, God, who is rich in mercy, made us alive with Christ even when we were dead in transgressions—it is by grace you have been saved.* (Eph. 2:4–5)

Prayer:

Reflection:

# Hope

How painful life can be as we learn and grow.
How hard it is to see beyond our pain when it overwhelms all
we feel, see, and know.
It is then we need the hand of grace to pull us out of the pain,
To know there is hope and
That the pain can be endured.
There is hope beyond the pain,
Beyond the tears.
We must realize we cannot go on alone
When pain is all we feel.
We must hold on tighter than we have ever held on before.
It is in these times that we will be overwhelmed
By the depth of the love our God has for us and
The lengths he will go to reach us.
All we have to do is to allow him to enter into our pain,
To help carry our burdens, and
Then we will be overwhelmed by his love—
No longer alone,
Lost in our pain.

*The LORD is good, a refuge in times of trouble. He cares for those who trust in him.* (Nah. 1:7)

Prayer:


Reflection:

*The Sun Will Rise Despite the Darkness*

Under the dark rubble of our lives shines a light that will strengthen us,
Giving us the courage to break through the darkness of our lives.
Only in this light will we receive the power to break through the darkness,
Being set free from that which oppresses us,
To be the person we are destined to be.

*This is the message we have heard from him and declare to you: God is light; In him there is no darkness at all. If we claim to have fellowship with him yet walk in the darkness we lie and do not live by the truth.* (1 John 1:5–7)

Prayer:

Reflection:

There are circumstances in life we just do not understand.
The days are difficult and dark, and
Hope is shattered.
Where is God?
We must make a choice:
To choose to have faith and believe our God is still in control,
To choose to believe our God loves beyond our understanding,
To choose to believe our God is greater than our present circumstances,
To choose to believe what we do not understand and cannot comprehend,
He will use all things for good.
It is at this place we must stand,
Remembering his faithfulness to us
To those who are his,
Over centuries past..
Although we do not understand,
We must hold onto that which is greater than this world,
For he has promised to be with us when we are weary and burdened,
When our dreams have shattered.
We are never alone;
He will never leave us.
We must cling to the promises of our God.
Then we will understand that our hope comes not from this world—
Our hope lies in him.

*Because God has said "Never will I leave you; never will I forsake you." So we can say with confidence, "The Lord is my helper, I will not be afraid. What can man do to me?"* (Heb. 13:5–6)

Prayer:

Reflection:

We wonder how our lives have become so dark and empty.
We need only look as far as our self-absorption and selfish desires,
For it is when we realize it is not about us at all
The dawn will come.
Our hope lies not in us—
It lies in him.

*Command those who are rich in this present world not to be arrogant nor to put their hope in wealth which is so uncertain, but to put their hope in God, who richly provides us with everything for our enjoyment. Command them to do good, to be rich in good deeds, and to be generous and willing to share. In this way they will lay up treasure for themselves as a firm foundation for the coming age, so that they may take hold of the life that is truly life.* (1 Tim. 6:17–19)

Prayer:

Reflection:

Through his love we can break down the walls that surround us,
Through love he shows us hope and forgiveness,
So we may see the possibilities—
A new life,
One that shares hope, love, and forgiveness to others.
As we reach out to others, we must comfort them with the same comforting love,
Allowing them to see the hope that is in him.

*Praise be to the God and Father of our Lord Jesus Christ, the Father of compassion and the God of all comfort, who comforts us in all our troubles, so that we can comfort those in any trouble with the comfort we ourselves have received from God. For just as the sufferings of Christ flow over into our lives, so also through Christ our comfort overflows. If we are distressed, it is for your comfort and salvation; if we are comforted, it is for your comfort, which produces in you patient endurance of the same sufferings we suffer.* (2 Cor. 1:3–7)

Prayer:


Reflection:

Because of you
The sun shines brighter,
There is hope for tomorrow,
My fear subsides,
I am stronger, and
I am free.

*He gives strength to the weary and increases the power of the weak.* (Isa. 40:29)

Prayer:

Reflection:

# Truth

> Within your reach,
> Within your grasp,
> Is the Truth,
> Freeing you from fear,
> Opening your heart to the freedom that lies within.

*To the Jews who had believed him, Jesus said, "If you hold to my teaching, you are really my disciples. Then you will know the truth, and the truth will set you free."* (John 8:31–32)

Prayer:

Reflection:

The endless search for truth reveals to us the fears that hold
us captive,
Suppressing who we are.
It is through this search for truth that the doors of understanding will be opened,
Releasing us from fear and
Freeing us to love.

*For the law was given through Moses; grace and truth came through Jesus Christ.* (John 1:17)

Prayer:

Reflection:

Only when we discard the cloaks of self-fulfillment and pride will truth be revealed.

*If we claim to have fellowship with him yet walk in the darkness we lie and do not live by the truth.* (1 John 1:6)

Prayer:

Reflection:

Foolish are we to assume to know the response of our God,
    For as soon as we assume the response,
        He will break through and reveal a greater truth.

*Call to me and I will answer you and tell you great and unsearchable things you do not know.* (Jer. 33:3)

Prayer:

Reflection:

# Wisdom

Wisdom is gained
By the relentless pursuit of that which we cannot find on our own
But know is there.
We must look beyond ourselves to find true wisdom,
For the answers will never be found when we are looking
through our own eyes.
It is only through the eyes of one far greater than ourselves
That wisdom will be revealed.

*I guide you in the way of wisdom and lead you along straight paths.*
(Prov. 4:11–12)

Prayer:

Reflection:

The greatest roadblock to wisdom is pride.
One must be humble to receive wisdom and remain humble to keep wisdom.

*For the LORD gives wisdom, and from his mouth come knowledge and understanding.* (Prov. 2:6)

Prayer:

Reflection:

Only when you walk with me will you soar like eagles above the clouds,
Reaching new heights of understanding and wisdom.
Only when you walk with me can you break through walls that surround you.
Only when you walk with me can you grasp the power that can set you free.
Only when you seek with an open heart will the truth be made known to you.

*But those who hope in the LORD will renew their strength. They will soar on wings like eagles; they will run and not grow weary, they will walk and not be faint.* (Isa. 40:31)

Prayer:

Reflection:

# Peace

*The Sun Will Rise Despite the Darkness*

As chaos swarms around our lives,
We are unable to hear the smallest of sounds.
We have forgotten the peace that silence brings.
We must stop and be still to hear our God;
It is in this silence we will know his voice.
As the soft voice of our Lord enters in,
Shattering the chaos,
We will receive the peace we so desire,
Focusing our lives beyond ourselves
To a purpose greater than our own.

*Be still, and know that I am God; I will be exalted among the nations, I will be exalted in the earth.* (Ps. 46:10)

Prayer:

Reflection:

Only in the quiet presence of our God will we find truth,
Restoring faith and hope and
Showing us abundant love.
It is this love that will carry us through the waves of uncertainty and fear,
For in this love there is no end—
There is peace.

*For I am the LORD, your God, who takes hold of your right hand and says to you, Do not fear; I will help you. Do not be afraid, O worm Jacob.* (Isa. 41:13)

Prayer:

Reflection:

*The Sun Will Rise Despite the Darkness*

In our longing for peace, we search everywhere
Except the one place peace can be found:
Through Jesus Christ.
We will only find true peace when we choose to forget the
self we would like to be
And understand the self we really are.

*I have told you these things, so that in me you may have peace. In this world you will have trouble. But take heart! I have overcome the world.* (John 16:33)

Prayer:

Reflection:

# Guidance

*The Sun Will Rise Despite the Darkness*

Gently the Lord guides us,
Knowing what we do not know—
For we are unable to understand the greatness of his plans—
Pushing us when we are unwilling,
Comforting us when we are fearful.
Always loving, never absent,
Along this journey he will change us.
It is the journey that is important.
Whether we allow him to be the guide is the greatest question.
When we choose Jesus, we find a path that can never be equaled.
In choosing him we will never look back and wish we had chosen ourselves.

*Show me your ways, O LORD, teach me your paths; guide me in your truth and teach me, for you are God my Savior, and my hope is in you all day long.* (Ps. 25:4–5)

Prayer:

Reflection:

At times you are called to follow a path that is unlike the one you would have chosen.
Instead, smooth, paved path may turn rocky and difficult to navigate.
You may feel it is too hard,
Too challenging—that
You are unable to travel on this path under your own strength.
You are right.
It is too difficult to navigate on your own skills and knowledge.
You must look to Jesus to be your guide through the challenging times.
You will never have the wisdom and understanding on your own.
Trust in him.
He has not chosen this path for you to follow to have you turn back mid-journey.
The question is, can you look beyond the current hardship,
Trusting there is a purpose?
Do you believe in your heart that Jesus will never leave you
Midst the rocky terrain of this uncertain place?
Keep focused on your guide and not on the conditions that surround you;
He has not taken you this far to abandon you.
The conditions on the path will change and be uncertain,
But Jesus will remain unchanged, no matter what you encounter on the journey.
He will supply all you need.
Will you be faithful in the uncertainty?

*Being confident of this, that he who began a good work in you will carry it on to completion until the day of Christ Jesus.* (Phil. 1:6)

Prayer:

Reflection:

In my effort to walk with you,
I find
I cannot walk apart from you.

*When Jesus spoke again to the people, he said, "I am the light of the world. Whoever follows me will never walk in darkness, but will have the light of life."* (John 8:12)

Prayer:

Reflection:

*The Sun Will Rise Despite the Darkness*

In the darkness of our lives,
When hopes are shattered,
Let the light guide you through the darkness,
Showing you the way,
Restoring hope.
When we are lost and
Unable to see,
There is one who will provide strength to break through the darkness,
Guiding us so that we may see.

*I will lead the blind by ways they have not known, along unfamiliar paths I will guide them. I will turn the darkness into light before them and make the rough places smooth. These are the things I will do; I will not forsake them.* (Isa. 42:16)

Prayer:

Reflection:

As we walk out of darkness into the light,
His power will set us free.
In our weakness,
He is strong.
What we do not know,
He knows.
What we do not see,
He sees.
As the path becomes rocky,
He will guide us.
When the path is impassable,
He will carry us.
Let no storm carry you off course.
Let God be your guide,
For he knows the path
You must follow.
Just hold out your hand, and follow him.

*The LORD will guide you always; he will satisfy your needs in a sunscorched land and will strengthen your frame. You will be like a well-watered garden, like a spring whose waters never fail.* (Isa. 58:11)

Prayer:

Reflection:

*The Sun Will Rise Despite the Darkness*

Believe in the power of the one who will set you free;
    He will set the course for you to follow.

*Indeed, in our hearts we felt the sentence of death. But this happened that we might not rely on ourselves but on God, who raises the dead.* (2 Cor. 1:9)

Prayer:

Reflection:

We must be willing to take the first step forward in faith,
Allowing our Lord to guide and protect us as we move forward.
As we increase our faith and trust in the Lord,
We will discover the life intended for us to lead.
Step forward in faith.

*For this God is our God forever and ever; he will be our guide even to the end.* (Ps. 48:14)

Prayer:

Reflection:

*The Sun Will Rise Despite the Darkness*

In the darkest moments of our lives, there shines a light,
Giving the courage we need,
Breaking through so we may begin the life that should be.
In the depths of our soul lies a restlessness,
A yearning
To understand a greater purpose.
It is only through relentless seeking that we will receive and be set free.

*But if from there you seek the LORD your God, you will find him if you look for him with all your heart and with all your soul.* (Deut. 4:29)

Prayer:

Reflection:

How well you know before I ask what I need.
How perfectly you guide me when I don't even know I'm lost.
How graciously you give me all that I need,
Even when I don't understand the depth of my need.
How wonderfully you restore and strengthen me,
Filling me with hope and love,
Reaching far beyond my understanding.
How grateful I am that you know me at all.

*Let us fix our eyes on Jesus, the author and perfecter of our faith, who for the joy set before him endured the cross, scorning its shame, and sat down at the right hand of the throne of God.* (Heb. 12:2)

Prayer:

Reflection:

*The Sun Will Rise Despite the Darkness*

Tossed by the waves of uncertainty
Onto an unfamiliar shore—
How did I arrive here?
Waves of mist and fog keep rolling in.
Seeking shelter.
Broken in spirit.
Desperately needing the light to burn through,
To calm the storm,
To be the compass.
Holding on, knowing I must ride out this storm,
Not understanding why.
But as I remember,
There has always been light above the fog.
And with me on this shore,
The light of love shines through,
The waves begin to subside,
The fog clears, and
Direction is provided
As I ask Jesus to enter in.

*Jacki Tase*

*Then Jesus told them this parable: Suppose one of you has a hundred sheep and losses one of them. Does he not leave the ninety-nine in the open country and go after the lost sheep until he finds it?* (Luke 15:3–4)

Prayer:


Reflection:

*The Sun Will Rise Despite the Darkness*

You have a choice
When the storms in your life begin to overwhelm you,
As the thunder dominates all other sound, so you cannot hear, and
The rain and fog distort your way.
You have a choice
When the waves of doubt begin to rock your foundation,
As the water rises and fears set in,
And hope sinks.
You have a choice:
Will you fight these storms alone,
Losing perspective as you lose yourself?
Or will you take the hand of the one who will give you shelter
from the storms,
Calming the fears,
Restoring the hope,
Showing you the way.
You have a choice.


*When Jesus spoke again to the people, he said, I am the light of the world. Whoever follows me will never walk in darkness, but will have the light of life.* (John 8:12)


Prayer:


Reflection:

# Letting Go

Our journey is lifelong
But limited by our inability to let go of that which holds us down.
When we are lost in our own desires, we cannot see the life that can be.
We may choose what is comfortable, known, and measurable, remaining unchanged,
Or choose what is immeasurable, infinite, and uncontainable and be changed forever.

*This is what the LORD says: "Stand at the crossroads and look; ask for the ancient paths, ask where the good way is and walk in it, and you will find rest for your souls." But you said, "We will not walk in it."* (Jer. 6:16)

Prayer:


Reflection:

We can let the setbacks in our lives define us, or we can use the setbacks as defining moments that awaken us to the better road that God has for us.

*"For I know the plans I have for you," declares the LORD, "plans to prosper you and not to harm you, plans to give you hope and a future. Then you will call on me and come and pray to me, and I will listen to you. You will seek me and find me when you seek me with all your heart. I will be found by you," declares the LORD.* (Jer. 29:11–14a)

Prayer:

Reflection:

*The Sun Will Rise Despite the Darkness*

The experience of loss is a unique opportunity
to learn new truths,
And gain understanding that is otherwise unattainable.
Loss forces us to look deeply within,
Forces us to change,
For we are no longer capable of identifying ourselves by what
we have lost.
Unable to fill the void on our own,
In the difficult process of letting go,
We have the opportunity to discover who we truly are.
The key is to be able to look beyond disillusionment,
Understanding how loss has changed our life—
What have you learned about yourself and others,
But most importantly
What have you learned about God.
Loss will change your perspective.
Look beyond yourself.
Allow it to change you.
Share it with others.
If you hold onto it for yourself,
You have not changed at all.

*What good is it for a man to gain the whole world, and yet lose or forfeit his very self?* (Luke 9:25)

Prayer:

Reflection:

# Change

As we reach out to others
And reach out to him,
We begin to be changed from within.

*Dear friends, since God so loved us, we also ought to love one another. No one has ever seen God; but if we love one another, God lives in us and his love is made complete in us.* (1 John 4:11–12)

Prayer:

Reflection:

It is our God who sends the Holy Spirit to begin to change us
from within,
So that we may then go forth,
Overcoming the great challenges standing before us and
Blocking our way—
Allowing us to go forth to fulfill our greater purpose.

*But when he, the Spirit of truth comes, he will guide you into all truth. He will not speak on his own; he will speak only what he hears, and he will tell you what is yet to come.* (John 16:13)

Prayer:

Reflection:

How painful it is to change and grow from what we are to
who we shall be.
How gracious our God is to carry us through the fear,
Changing us throughout the journey, and
Allowing us and others to see him.

*So do not fear, for I am with you; do not be dismayed, for I am your God. I will strengthen you and help you; I will uphold you with my righteous right hand.* (Isa. 41:10)

Prayer:

Reflection:

In life we will experience events that immobilize us, and we
ask, why
It is under this pressure that our self-reliance weakens,
Challenging us to rely on God
Because our old ways no longer work.
We need to realize we cannot move forward in our present
state.
We must allow God to change us, so we can move on.
If we choose to rely on him for our answers and direction,
We begin to be renewed.
We cannot effectively serve him
If we do not begin to change from who we are
To what he desires us to be.

*And he said; I tell you the truth, unless you change and become like little children, you will never enter the kingdom of heaven. Therefore, whoever humbles himself like this child is the greatest in the kingdom of heaven.* (Matt. 18:3–4)

Prayer:

Reflection:

*The Sun Will Rise Despite the Darkness*

Where you have been matters not to him—
It is where you stand today and
Where you are about to go that matters.

*Here I am! I stand at the door and knock. If anyone hears my voice and opens the door, I will come in and eat with him, and he with me.* (Rev. 3:20)

Prayer:

Reflection:

It is when our lives are filled with discontent
That we must look to our own selfish desires.
It is the focus on ourselves that distances us from God,
Causing us to look everywhere except to him for the answer.
We must change the focus of our lives from selfishness to selflessness.
In true love and service to others, our selfishness cannot exist.
It is the unselfish love of Jesus Christ that will rescue us from our discontent.
It is when we stop focusing on our needs and begin to focus on the needs of others
We learn the most about ourselves.

*Do nothing out of selfish ambition or vain conceit, but in humility consider others better than yourselves.* (Phil. 2:3)

Prayer:

Reflection:

# Faith

*The Sun Will Rise Despite the Darkness*

How hard is it to believe what is unseen against
that which is seen?
How hard is it to stand when others run?
How hard is it to believe in the midst of unbelief?
How hard is it to resist when the temptations are so strong?
How hard is it to be certain when uncertainty surrounds us?
How foolish are we if we believe we can stand alone?

*Now faith is being sure of what we hope for and certain of what we do not see.* (Heb. 11:1)

Prayer:

Reflection:

Only when you reach out will you see,
Grasping the truth,
Growing in faith.

*But grow in the grace and knowledge of our Lord and Savior Jesus Christ. To him be the glory both now and forever! Amen.* (2 Pet. 3:18)

Prayer:

Reflection:

# Feeling Alone

*The Sun Will Rise Despite the Darkness*

In the quiet and empty times, loneliness creeps in.
It hovers over even our busiest days
Like an unwelcomed visitor waiting in the wings,
Waiting for that vulnerable moment—
A memory of the past,
The uncertainty of the future,
The moment that shakes your faith.
In that quiet emptiness where uncertainty lives,
There is an unexpected moment presenting a choice:
To stay in the emptiness, the uncertainty,
Or to reach out to the only one who can fill the space—
The one who is willing to guide you out of the emptiness and uncertainty,
To give you a firm place to stand,
To begin to see and feel joy again.
Beginning to shed the unwanted loneliness,
Filling the emptiness with hope once more,
He is the Lord who will sustain you.
It is a choice:
To stay in the uncertainty or choose the certain way, the certain path.
Take one step today, restoring the fullness and joy,
Restoring the faith.
Come, Lord Jesus, come!

*Surely God is my help. The LORD is the one who sustains me.* (Ps. 54:4)


Prayer:


Reflection:

*The Sun Will Rise Despite the Darkness*

In our darkest hour,
When silence is deafening
And we are isolated in our pain,
God is there.
In that moment he will hear our cry.
We need to reach out for the strength we do not have,
Acknowledging his greatness and accepting his grace.
In that moment we will know
We are not alone,
For he is our God.

*The LORD is the refuge for the oppressed, a stronghold in times of trouble. Those who know your name will trust in you, for you, LORD, have never forsaken those who seek you.* (Ps. 9:9–10)

Prayer:

Reflection:

*Jacki Tase*

In the quiet stillness of the morning,
I humbly come before you,
Revealing my inadequacies and burdens,
Exposing the cold, empty pain and my longing for you.
In that moment you blanket me with your love and mercy,
Filling the emptiness,
Healing the pain,
Preparing me for another day.
Strengthened by your love,
Which gives me hope in you,
Knowing you are always with me,
I am not alone.

*It is God who arms me with strength and makes my way perfect.* (Ps. 18:23)

Prayer:

Reflection:

# Grief

*The Sun Will Rise Despite the Darkness*

Grief gently settles into the heart,
With a quiet hush of sadness and
An unrelenting heaviness,
Catching you unaware,
Blurring perspective,
Numbing you to the joys of life,
Slowly drowning out hope.
But beneath the layers of gray,
All hope is not lost.
There is the Lord's gentle breath
Pouring hope into your heart,
Piece by piece, over time.
The healing light will pierce the numbness,
Pushing the darkness away.
It is the Lord, the Holy One,
Who enters in,
Removing each layer,
Soothing the pain,
Restoring your grief-filled heart.
To see hope and love clearly once more,
Open your heart to the healing power of his glorious light.

*Find rest, O my soul, in God alone; my hope comes from him.* (Ps. 62:5)

Prayer:

Reflection:

# When God Seems Silent

*The Sun Will Rise Despite the Darkness*

There are moments in our lives when it is difficult to praise God,
Seeing no reason for praise.
We get lost in a dark, empty, hopeless fog of despair.
It is in moments such as these
We must do what we have forgotten to do:—
Remember to praise God
For who he is,
Who he has been,
And who he will always be;
Understand we may never understand
Why life is, as it is, at this moment;
Allow ourselves to be loved and
Sheltered by him;
Trusting,
Loving,
Being thankful even when we feel God has been silent.
We must remember who we are:
Children of God.
In this moment of silence,
This moment of despair,
He has not forgotten us.
The question is,
Have we forgotten him?

*Hear my cry, O God; listen to my prayer. From the ends of the earth I call to you, I call as my heart grows faint; lead me to the rock that is higher than I. For you have been my refuge, a strong tower against the foe. I long*

*to dwell in your tent forever and take refuge in the shelter of your wings.*
(Ps. 61:1–4)


Prayer:


Reflection:

# Obedience

*The Sun Will Rise Despite the Darkness*

In our efforts to understand God,
We diminish who he is in our minds by trying to understand in our finite ways.
We must open ourselves to the possibility
That we will never fully understand who he is.
It is when we feel we know and understand him that we do not know him at all.
The key does not lie in whether we understand.
It lies in our obedience.

*Blessed are they who keep his statutes and seek him with all their heart.* (Ps. 119:2)

Prayer:

Reflection:

Experiences and gifts are given to further kingdom purposes,
not our own purposes.
They are not our goals but his goals,
Not our wants but his wants.
It is not for us to decide what is important.
What is important is that we follow his Word,
Listening to our hearts as well as our minds.

*For I have come down from heaven not to do my will but to do the will of him who sent me.* (John 6:38)

Prayer:

Reflection:

*The Sun Will Rise Despite the Darkness*

> Standing firm,
> Comforted by faith,
> Unwilling to give up,
> Developing a faith that is patient,
> Tirelessly pushing forward,
> Desiring Jesus above all else—
> Go forth and serve.

*And now, O Israel, what does the LORD your God ask of you but to fear the LORD your God, to walk in all his ways, to love him, to serve the LORD your God with all your heart and with all your soul, and to observe the LORD's commands and decrees that I am giving you today for your own good.* (Deut. 10:12–13)

Prayer:

Reflection:

# Purpose

*The Sun Will Rise Despite the Darkness*

We spend a great deal of our lives looking for our purpose and
The meaning of our lives.
Much of our lives we are driven to find where we belong.
It is not until we realize we are God's children, understand
We are his,
The searching ends.
It is then the peace of knowing, understanding, and belonging
is fulfilled.
His love is there for us, just as we are,
Fulfilling all of our needs.
There are no special accomplishments, degrees, or rungs in
the ladder to climb,
He loves us now.
We are his children.
Let us be grateful for who we are and open our hears to all his
children,
Loving as he loves us.
Let us worship him for who he is—
Our Father and our God.

*Come, let us bow down in worship, let us kneel before the LORD our Maker, for he is our God and we are the people of his pasture, the flock under his care.* (Ps. 95:6–7)


Prayer:


Reflection:

*The Sun Will Rise Despite the Darkness*

It has happened over time.
At what point, I am not sure, but
Within my heart I have come to understand
Your desire is only for me:
My will, heart, and praise;
My worship, tears, and joys;
My all.
Nothing less, nothing more.
To surrender my will and dreams,
To accept yours instead…
At what point, I am not sure, but
I began to understand
The joy this brings
A deeper love,
Peace within my soul,
Subtle strength, and
A compassionate heart.
At what point, I am not sure, but
I began to see the world differently:
To see the heartache, despair, and hunger,
The need for hope,
The need for love—
To hear the cries of those who wonder,
Does someone even care?
It is time to hear those cries,
To reach out and hold,
To comfort, love, and offer hope.

We have not been given this knowledge and this peace to
hold, but to share.
He did not come for just one; he came for all.

*For great is your love towards me, you have delivered me from the depths of the grave. But you, O Lord, are a compassionate and gracious God.* (Ps. 86:13, 15)

Prayer:

Reflection:

We spend our lives striving for those things—
Achievements to boost our egos,
Our feelings of self-worth.
In this life of self-fulfillment, we have missed the point.
Our true purpose is to put aside our personal goals and take on kingdom goals—
To be able to be used for the benefits of the kingdom,
For purposes unknown to us.

*But seek first his kingdom and his righteousness and all these things will be given to you as well.* (Matt. 6:33)

Prayer:

Reflection:

It is when we admit our weaknesses,
Our pride and selfish desires—
Submitting to who you are,
We find who we can be.

*Humble yourselves before the Lord, and he will lift you up.* (James 4:10)

Prayer:

Reflection:

*The Sun Will Rise Despite the Darkness*

I come to you searching for a life with meaning;
I have been lost in my own selfish desires.
I come to you with an emptiness I am unable to fill on my own.
I come to you seeking understanding and a better way,
And as I come to you, I discover
I will never understand until I leave me behind and come to you.

*Do nothing out of selfish ambition or vain conceit, but in humility consider others better than yourselves.* (Phil. 2:3)

Prayer:

Reflection:

What if we are wrong?
What if the path to success is not in what we achieve for ourselves,
But in what we help others achieve?
What if success is not determined by
The money you make, the clothes you wear, the people you know, and
The status you achieve
But rather by the people you feed, the children you love, and
The lives you change by the hope you give?
What if our days were guided by caring more instead of accumulating more?
What if we built up others instead of building up ourselves?
What if tomorrow wasn't nearly as important as today?
What if we are wrong?

*Do not store up for yourselves treasures on earth, where moth and rust destroy, and where thieves break in and steal. But store up for yourselves treasures in heaven, where moth and rust do not destroy, and where thieves do not break in and steal. For where your treasure is, there your heart will be also.* (Matt. 6:19–21)

Prayer:


Reflection:

*The Sun Will Rise Despite the Darkness*

How long can we be silent
As darkness weaves itself into our lives, surrounding
us with pain?
How long can we be silent
As our children die and those who remain cry out in fear,
Not understanding how we do not hear?
How long can we be silent
As the light begins to fade and hopelessness begins to reign?
How long can we be silent?
As long as we are silent,
Darkness will grow and hope will die.

*Is not this the kind of fasting I have chosen: to loose the chains of injustice and untie the cords of the yoke, to set the oppressed free and break every yoke? Is it not to share your food with the hungry and to provide the poor wanderer with shelter—when you see the naked, to clothe him, and not to turn away from your own flesh and blood?* (Isa. 58:6)

Prayer:

Reflection:

To hear as he hears,
To see as he sees,
To forgive as he has forgiven,
To be obedient as he was obedient,
To love as he loves—
This is to be all that we are meant to be.

*Whoever claims to live in him must walk as Jesus did.* (1 John 2:6)

Prayer:

Reflection:

Learning,
Hearing,
Doing—
Unsuccessful in isolation,
Unstoppable in unison.

*You see that his faith and his actions were working together, and his faith was made complete by what he did.* (James 2:22)

Prayer:

Reflection:

There is a watching world that watches you and me
To see if what we say we believe can actually be.
Does it see the possibility, hope, joy, and love?
Or does it see a disconnect in the life we lead and the one we speak of?
If we do not live as we speak, love as we act, and help when there is need,
How can those who are watching believe what they do not see?
Will our God's love be real if they never feel his love from you and me?
Are we too busy to hear, too hurried to care, too self-focused to see
The need that is there?
Too afraid, too powerless, and too tired to know
There is a world that needs to see and a world that needs to know?
The answer must be reflected in your life and mine
To show there is an answer, a power, hope, love,
A place to be known, and a place to be,
If only we would do as we say and live as it can be.
So take a long look at the life that you lead.
Does your life reflect the love, hope, joy, and kindness we say can be?
As the watching world looks on, it will see
A reflection of Jesus in you and in me.
The love will be real—
The answer is there.
Only then will there be a desire to reach out and grasp what has always been there.

*You are the light of the world, a city on a hill cannot be hidden. Neither do people light a lamp and put it under a bowl. Instead they put it on its stand, and it gives a light to everyone in the house. In the same way let your light shine before men, that they see your good deeds and praise your Father in heaven.* (Matt. 5:14–16)

Prayer:

Reflection:

# Seeking God

Let us not forget who God is in our desire to do his will.
We must always question exactly whose will it is.
Is it the desire for recognition of one's self,
Or is it for one greater?
Let us never forget that it is for God's glory,
For if it is not for God's glory,
It is not God's will;
It is ours.

*Declare his glory among the nations, his marvelous deeds among all peoples. For great is the LORD and most worthy of praise; he is to be feared above all gods. For all the gods of the nations are idols, but the LORD made the heavens. Splendor and majesty are before him; strength and glory are in his sanctuary.* (Ps. 96:3–6)

Prayer:

Reflection:

There is a tendency in our culture to rush to the next thing,
To push forward, never taking time to live in this moment.
By doing so we miss the gift of the moment, this day, this time.
The true gift is to embrace the now—take hold of today.
Tomorrow is truly not ours to take.
What is the gift that our Lord has for us now?
Will we miss it because we are so focused on what may or may not be?
Take the time to reflect upon today.
What wonderful gift has God unfolded
before you in this day?
Can you see it?
Do you have eyes opened and a heart ready to receive it,
Or is your attention focused elsewhere—on that which may never be?
Live in this day, this moment.
Let it unfold before you.
Be ready to receive the gift of God's love.

*Therefore I tell you, do not worry about your life, what you will eat or drink; or about your body, what you will wear. Is not life more important than food, and the body more important than clothes? Look at the birds of the air; they do not sow or reap or store away in barns, and yet our heavenly Father feeds them. Are you not much more valuable than they? Who of you by worrying can add a single hour to his life? Seek first his (God's) kingdom and his righteousness.* (Matt. 6:25–34)

Prayer:

Reflection:

# Following Jesus

*The Sun Will Rise Despite the Darkness*

What kind of life will you lead
Once you have been given the power to see?
The darkness is relentless, and the battles loom before you,
Leaving so many to be healed.
Will you lead a life of faith and trust,
Allowing the past to fade and the future to be?
It is a time of decision,
For in the end it is only love that will remain.

*For God did not give us a spirit of timidity, but a spirit of power, of love and of self-discipline.* (2 Tim. 1:7)

Prayer:

Reflection:

Are you willing
To obey without complete understanding,
To leave behind what is comfortable for what is unknown,
To see life from an eternal perspective,
To delay your rewards?
Are you willing
To stand firm when others falter,
To reach out to others without question,
To put aside your plans for a plan much greater,
To follow him no matter what the cost?
Are you willing?

*Whoever serves me must follow me; and where I am, my servant also will be. My Father will honor the one who serves me.* (John 12:26)

Prayer:

Reflection:

*The Sun Will Rise Despite the Darkness*

Consumed with the desire—
A fire within—
To reach out beyond
Comfort and safety,
To share the truth
With an open heart,
To stand back and watch
As God steps in,
Changing a life.
Just share the Word,
Step back, and see.
He will set them free.

*Then you will know the truth, and the truth will set you free.* (John 8:32)

Prayer:

Reflection:

# Fear

*The Sun Will Rise Despite the Darkness*

In the uncertainty,
In the seeking of your will…
Jesus, fill me with a passion and desire for you—
One that will drown out the doubt,
One that will extinguish the fear.
My heart's desire is to know you
And to serve you with joy.

*Strengthen the feeble hands, steady the knees that give way; say to those with fearful hearts, be strong, don't fear, your God will come with vengeance with divine retribution, he will come to save you.* (Isa. 35:3–4)

Prayer:

Reflection:

*Jacki Tase*

Fear builds a wall that isolates us from our God.
The more fear we have,
The greater the wall becomes,
Until we feel isolated and alone.
We begin to feel God is not there,
Feel he does not hear us, that
He is not providing for us.
This is the deception of fear.
We must believe God is with us.
He hears our cries.
We must reach out in faith to begin to weaken the wall of fear that surrounds us.
As we do we will gain confidence and knowledge that, yes, God is here.
He will strengthen us.
He will provide for us.
As he does, our faith will grow;
The walls will begin to crumble, and
We will no longer be deceived into believing our God does not hear.
The power to begin to break down the walls built on fear is here for us now.
His love will give us the strength required to overcome the fear,
For our God is not a God of fear and isolation—
Our God is a God of freedom and love.

*But now, this is what the LORD says—he who created you, O Jacob, he who formed you, O Israel: Fear not, for I have redeemed you; I have summoned you by name; you are mine. When you pass through the waters, I will be with you; and when you pass through the rivers, they will not sweep over you. When you walk through the fire, you will not be burned; the flames will not set you ablaze. For I am the LORD, your God, the Holy One of Israel, your Savior; I give Egypt for your ransom, Cush and Seba in your stead. Since you are precious and honored in my sight and because I love you I will give men in exchange for you, and people in exchange for your life. Do not be afraid, for I am with you.* (Isa. 43:1–5)

Prayer:

Reflection:

# Strength

*The Sun Will Rise Despite the Darkness*

When the winds of life try to blow you off course,
How firm is your hold on Jesus?
It is easy to hold on in calm winds.
But as the wind begins to increase and change,
Will your efforts to hold on increase as well?
Will you let go when the effort needed to hold on begins to overpower you,
Or will you just let go because the battle to hold on is too great?
We must do all we can to hold on in those storms, for it will require greater effort.
As we struggle to hold on, we must remember what we know is true.
There is security in knowing Jesus,
He will strengthen us when we are tired of holding on.
He will carry us through the storms.
How strongly will you hold on?
Can your faith withstand the winds that will come your way?
How firmly anchored are you in the Word of God?
How relentless are you in prayer?
When the winds are strong and unceasing,
It will be the Word of God,
Prayer, and your relationship with Jesus Christ that will sustain you,
Giving the hope and strength needed to hold on.
So when the winds of life begin to blow strong,
Will you hold on?

*Let us hold unswervingly to the hope we profess for he who promised is faithful.* (Heb. 10:23)

Prayer:

Reflection:

*The Sun Will Rise Despite the Darkness*

In the quiet of the morning, I come to you,
Knowing my weakness,
Seeing my failings,
Wondering what the day has in store,
Seeking guidance,
Needing focus,
Wondering how I will do all that is before me.

Then, in the quiet of the morning,
I understand deep within my heart
It is not on my own strength that I go.
As dawn approaches I realize
I do not need to be concerned about these things,
For the one who has created the dawn is the one whose strength I need.
This is not something I need to muster up;
Rather, it is something that is available to me.
I am grateful for and to receive this gift.

In the quiet of the morning, I come to you.
I am strengthened,
Given hope, and encouraged,
Understanding that whatever is in store—
Whatever lies before me—
Is not impossible for the one who has created the dawn.
May the God of creation strengthen, uphold, and guide me on this day.

*In my anguish I cried to the LORD and he answered by setting me free. I will not die but live and will proclaim what the LORD has done.* (Ps. 118:5, 17)

Prayer:

Reflection:

*The Sun Will Rise Despite the Darkness*

In my weakness and pain,
I fall to my knees,
Unable to take another step.
Knowing at this moment
I can no longer walk alone,
I cry out to you, and you are there
Showering me with forgiveness,
Strengthening me from within,
Showing me a greater love.
I realize that with you I can walk through this pain,
Gaining strength and a greater understanding of who you are,
Knowing who I am and what I am meant to be.

*God is our refuge and strength, and ever present help in trouble.* (Ps. 46:1)

Prayer:

Reflection:

# Trusting God

*The Sun Will Rise Despite the Darkness*

There are times that our burden is great:
The weight we carry seems heavy upon our shoulders, and
We are weary and tired.
It may be a burden we carry for ourselves
Or one that we carry for others.
On those days that the weight is too heavy,
Remember there is one that walks with you,
Willing to carry the burden.
The weight may remain for a time,
But there is relief in knowing
There is one who knows,
Who sees, and
Who hears,
One who will not allow us to break,
even when the pressure is great.
Have confidence, and know
You are not alone.
Have confidence, and know
He is your God.
Cry out, for Jesus hears.
Cry out, for Jesus loves.
Cry out, for Jesus has not forgotten.

*I waited patiently for the LORD; He turned to me and heard my cry. He lifted me out of the slimy pit, out of the mud and mire; he set my feet on a rock and gave me a firm place to stand.* (Ps. 40:1–2)

Prayer:

Reflection:

Our need for instant answers prevents us from seeing the true work of God.
It is necessary for us to be patient,
Allowing God to work.
Our impatience demonstrates
Our lack of trust and faith that God is in control.

*He who trusts in himself is a fool, but he who walks in wisdom is kept safe.* (Prov. 28:26)

Prayer:

Reflection:

Trusting in the power of the Word and
Believing in the strength it brings
Will lead you down the path that is the life you have been
destined for.
You must be willing to believe that
Power and strength will be provided as you move on this path.
Believe in the Word given to you.

*I was pushed back and about to fall, but the LORD is my strength and my song; he has become my salvation.* (Ps. 118:13–14)

Prayer:

Reflection:

*The Sun Will Rise Despite the Darkness*

When the day is long and
The path seems dark,
Will I trust in you
Even then?

When the direction seems unclear and
The daily battle looms large,
Will I follow you
Even then?

When I am thirsty and the well seems dry and
The journey seems too hard,
Will I praise you
Even then?

When I wonder why and
My eyes seem never to be dry,
Will I love you
Even then?

When the answer never comes and
I feel so afraid,
Will I thank you
Even then?

When I am on my knees day after day and
Peace never seems to come,
Will I still seek you
Even then?

When what you provided is far different
Than I thought I would need,
Will I still be grateful
Even then?

When the lesson is hard
And I just do not understand,
Can my heart be filled with gratitude
Even then?

Yes, even then
I will thank you.
When the answers never seem to come
And the water never flows,
I will be grateful in this place.

Yes, even then
I will trust in you.
When the path ahead is unclear
And peace has not come,
I will trust you in this place.

We must learn how to trust in you,
When the days are filled with challenges—
Learn to see the world through your eyes
And love as you do,
Whether it is a time of abundance
Or a time of great need.

*The Sun Will Rise Despite the Darkness*

> Yes, even then
> I will trust in you,
> Follow you, and
> I will love you, Jesus—
> Even then!

*Surely God is my salvation; I will trust and not be afraid. The LORD, the LORD, is my strength and my song; he has become my salvation.* (Isa. 12:2)

Prayer:

Reflection:

# Author biography

Jacki Tase grew up attending church with her family but drifted away as she reached early adulthood. It wasn't until many years later that the reality of a personal relationship with Christ and submission to his authority completely changed her life.

Jacki received a bachelor's degree from Eastern University. She then earned her master's degree in religion, specializing in biblical studies from Evangelical Theological Seminary in Myerstown, Pennsylvania.

Jacki has served in a variety of ministry settings, often speaking at retreats and leadership events. Currently, Jacki is on staff at the Church of the Good Samaritan in Paoli, Pennsylvania. She and her husband live in the suburbs of Philadelphia and have two wonderful daughters.